PETER COOK · LAURA SUZUKI

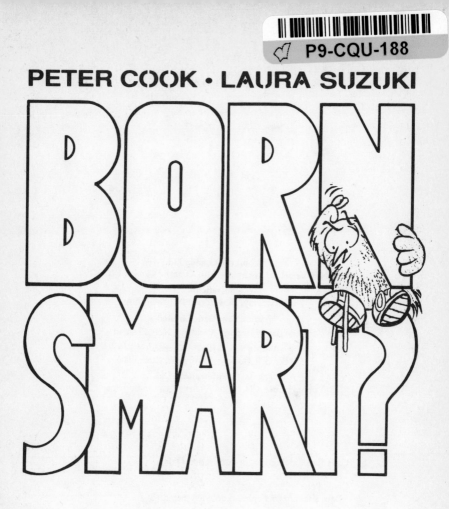

BORN SMART?

WHY ANIMALS DO WHAT THEY DO

Scholastic Canada Ltd.

Scholastic Canada Ltd.
123 Newkirk Road, Richmond Hill, Ontario, Canada L4C 3G5
Scholastic Inc.
730 Broadway, New York, NY 10003, USA
Ashton Scholastic Limited
Private Bag 1, Penrose, Auckland, New Zealand
Ashton Scholastic Pty Limited
PO Box 579, Gosford, NSW 2250, Australia
Scholastic Publications Ltd.
Villiers House, Clarendon Avenue, Leamington Spa,
Warwickshire CV32 5PR, UK

Canadian Cataloguing in Publication Data

Cook, Peter, 1965-
  Born smart? : why animals do what they do

ISBN O-590-74770-3

I. Instinct — Juvenile literature. 2. Animal behavior — Juvenile
literature. I. Suzuki, Laura. II. Title.

QL781.C66 1993   j591.51   C93-093419-9

6 5 4 3 2 1   Printed in Canada   3 4 5/9

To David T. Suzuki
for helping us get our foot
(feet?) in the door...

Many thanks to:
Dr. Chris Clark, Cornell University
Richard Johnstone, Metropolitan Toronto Zoo
Toby Styles, Metropolitan Toronto Zoo
Dr. Mason Weinrich, Cetacean Research Institute

TABLE OF CONTENTS

WHY DO ANIMALS ACT THE WAY THEY DO?

What makes moths fly in circles around light bulbs?

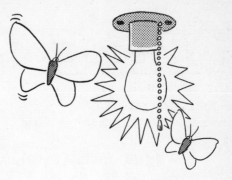

Why does your dog (well, some people's dogs) drool when it sees you opening a can of food?

Why do armadillos bash their heads on the grilles and undersides of cars and trucks?

And megapodes. How does this family of birds (whose name is Greek for "huge feet") know what to do as parents? Instead of sitting on their eggs, most megapodes make a mound of warm, rotting plants and earth to lay their eggs in.

The father works on the heap every day, checking the temperature with his beak, then adding or removing material. This keeps it at just the right warmth for the eggs.

When the eggs hatch, the chicks dig themselves out and walk away, hardly noticed by the father, who's busy with the pile. The chick is on its own and never sees its parents again. And yet, when it's grown up and has eggs to take care of, it will know exactly what to do!

How does it do this?

YEAH, HOW? AM I BORN SMART?

POP!

WELL, LET'S JUST SAY BORN WITH LOTS OF POTENTIAL...

LET'S START AT THE BEGINNING...

WHERE DOES AN ANIMAL'S BEHAVIOUR COME FROM?

A BEHAVIOUR CAN BE LEARNED FROM OUTSIDE EXPERIENCE OR ALREADY BE "BUILT-IN" INSIDE THE ANIMAL.

From the moment an animal is born...

OR HATCHES!

...it already has behaviours — it can do some things without ever being taught. Things like breaking an eggshell or sucking a nipple...

...OR LIVING WITHOUT ITS PARENTS' HELP, **HINT, HINT**...

As it grows up, it gets new behaviours that help it get through life. Some of them are so complicated that it's amazing that the animal doesn't have to learn them!

WHOA! I SUDDENLY FEEL LIKE MAKING A PILE OF ROTTING VEGGIES!

THESE BUILT-IN BEHAVIOURS ARE CALLED **INSTINCTS**. THE ANIMAL KNOWS WHEN, WHERE AND HOW TO DO THEM WITHOUT THINKING ABOUT IT.

THIS IS WEIRD...

INSTINCT

OOH! BIG WORD! BOOGIE! BOOGIE! BOOGIE!

THERE ARE DIFFERENT KINDS OF INSTINCT. THE SIMPLEST IS THE REFLEX.

A **reflex** is a quick action in direct response to an event (called a stimulus) happening to the animal.

HEY, WATCH IT!

A puff of air makes an animal's eye blink.

If you put a hand on a hot stove you yank it away quickly.

SSS

Many reflexes are so quick that they don't even go through the brain — the response would take too long if the signal had to go that far.

PULL

PAIN

SSSS

NO MORE FOR ME, THANKS.

A blowfly has a simple reflex to stop eating when its stomach is full.

If the nerve that sends the reflex signal stops working, the blowfly will eat until it explodes.

WELL, OKAY, JUST ONE MORE...

Other instinctive behaviours depend on a stimulus that is constantly there. If the stimulus goes away, the behaviour stops.

FOR EXAMPLE...

A stimulus can also trigger more complicated behaviours. These are called **action patterns** because the action is done in pretty much the same pattern each time.

FOR INSTANCE, IF A MOTHER GREYLAG GOOSE HAS AN EGG ROLL OUT OF THE NEST, SHE GOES THROUGH A PARTICULAR BEHAVIOUR PATTERN TO GET IT BACK.

BUT AN ACTION PATTERN CAN'T BE CHANGED. ONCE SHE STRETCHES HER NECK OUT, SHE'LL FOLLOW THAT PATTERN OF ROLLING THE EGG BACK...EVEN IF IT'S TAKEN AWAY!

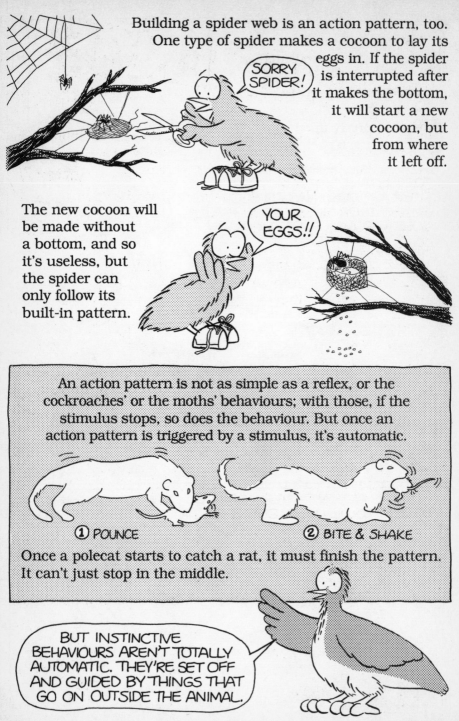

Building a spider web is an action pattern, too. One type of spider makes a cocoon to lay its eggs in. If the spider is interrupted after it makes the bottom, it will start a new cocoon, but from where it left off.

SORRY SPIDER!

The new cocoon will be made without a bottom, and so it's useless, but the spider can only follow its built-in pattern.

YOUR EGGS!!

An action pattern is not as simple as a reflex, or the cockroaches' or the moths' behaviours; with those, if the stimulus stops, so does the behaviour. But once an action pattern is triggered by a stimulus, it's automatic.

① POUNCE

② BITE & SHAKE

Once a polecat starts to catch a rat, it must finish the pattern. It can't just stop in the middle.

BUT INSTINCTIVE BEHAVIOURS AREN'T TOTALLY AUTOMATIC. THEY'RE SET OFF AND GUIDED BY THINGS THAT GO ON OUTSIDE THE ANIMAL.

EXPERIENCE

OW.

Everything around us has some effect on us. Even "built-in" behaviours can be changed by outside influences — the animal's surroundings and experiences.

WHAT?!

Turtle and crocodile hatchlings will develop into different sexes depending on the temperature of the sand the eggs are buried in. And that will change their behaviour for the rest of their lives.

YEAH, BUT WHAT ABOUT AFTER HATCHING?

EVEN THEN, SOME "AUTOMATIC" BEHAVIOURS CAN BE CHANGED BY YOUR SURROUNDINGS.

Male crickets have a built-in ability to chirp to attract female crickets.

CHIRP!

FRONT WINGS RUB TOGETHER

But even this "automatic" behaviour depends on the temperature of the air.

CHIRP CHIRP

CHIRP CHIRP CHIRP CHIRP CHIRP

But the main way outside experiences affect an animal's behavior is through **learning**.

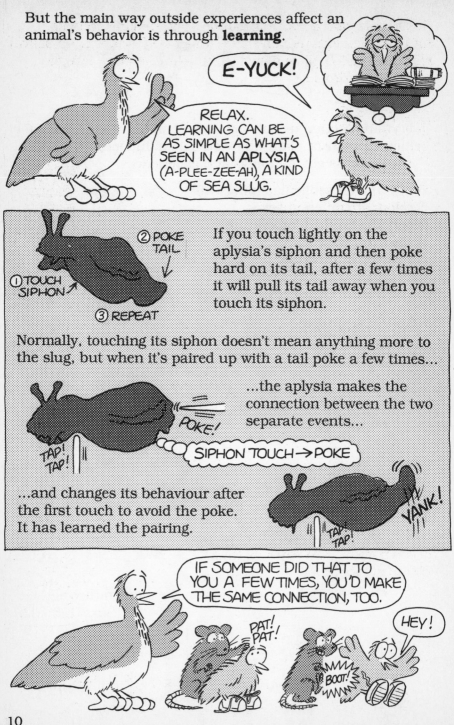

E-YUCK!

RELAX. LEARNING CAN BE AS SIMPLE AS WHAT'S SEEN IN AN **APLYSIA** (A-PLEE-ZEE-AH), A KIND OF SEA SLUG.

② POKE TAIL

① TOUCH SIPHON

③ REPEAT

If you touch lightly on the aplysia's siphon and then poke hard on its tail, after a few times it will pull its tail away when you touch its siphon.

Normally, touching its siphon doesn't mean anything more to the slug, but when it's paired up with a tail poke a few times...

...the aplysia makes the connection between the two separate events...

POKE!

TAP! TAP!

SIPHON TOUCH → POKE

...and changes its behaviour after the first touch to avoid the poke. It has learned the pairing.

TAP! TAP!

YANK!

IF SOMEONE DID THAT TO YOU A FEW TIMES, YOU'D MAKE THE SAME CONNECTION, TOO.

PAT! PAT!

HEY!

BOOT!

10

This simple paired learning can be seen in many animals. For example, dogs usually start to salivate (release extra saliva) when they're fed. (People do too, but they usually learn to swallow, not drool.)

SOME DOGS LEARN THAT THE SOUND OF A CAN OPENER MEANS *FOOD*, AND START TO SALIVATE EVEN BEFORE THEY SEE THEIR DINNER.

WHOA! NIAGARA FALLS!

Learning involves connecting one object or situation with another. Newly-hatched baby chicks will peck at anything small and roundish: corn, pebbles, other chicks' eyes, anything.

JUST YOU WATCH IT, BUSTER!

But a few days later, the chicks will only peck at things they know are food. And within a few more days, they can even learn pairings with different colours of food.

THE YELLOW CORN'S FINE, BUT THIS BLUE STUFF IS TERRIBLE!

If you raise some pigeons in a box so that they can't practise using their wings, then let them out...

THEY CAN FLY ABOUT AS WELL AS NORMAL PIGEONS!

FOR PIGEONS, THE ABILITY TO FLY DEPENDS ON MATURING RATHER THAN PRACTISING AND LEARNING.

IN HUMANS, TOO!

Traditionally, mothers of Arizona's Hopi people carried their babies strapped to boards on their backs.

THIS IS THE LIFE, I GUESS...

BOY, I'M GLAD I DIDN'T HAVE TWINS!

BABY WITH PRACTICE

BABY WITHOUT PRACTICE

Even though the babies didn't get much practice, they started walking at the same age as babies who'd practised a lot.

SO BABIES ONLY WALK WHEN THEY'RE GOOD AND READY!

BUT BACK TO LEARNING...

LEARNING AND INSTINCT USUALLY WORK TOGETHER.

THIS ALLOWS ANIMALS TO ADAPT TO DIFFERENT SITUATIONS.

A galah is a bird in the parrot family that often shares the nest of another parrot, the pink cockatoo. Sometimes the cockatoos end up raising the galahs' chicks.

GALAH

PINK COCKATOO

The chicks grow up thinking they're cockatoos. And though they keep some built-in behaviours — they beg for food as chicks and give alarm calls in the galah way — they call like, fly like, and hang around with pink cockatoos. Learning lets the galah adapt.

BUT TO LEARN ANYTHING, YOU NEED EXPERIENCE.

Kittens and baby wild cats naturally show stalking and attacking behaviours, but they don't know instinctively how to catch and kill prey. They learn by watching their parents.

And by trying it themselves....

THE WAY MOST YOUNG MAMMALS GET THEIR PRACTICE IS BY PLAYING.

Young animals explore, run, stalk, chase and flee, catch and get caught, and get a lot of experience in the things they'll need to do as adults. Play is practice for the real thing.

SO IS THE LEARNING MORE IMPORTANT THAN INSTINCT?

THE LEARNING IS A BIG PART, BUT IT'S THE BUILT-IN BEHAVIOURS THAT **GUIDE** WHAT IS LEARNED.

Chicks hatch with an instinctive pecking behaviour, but they have to learn how and when to use it. Kittens have a built-in desire to hunt and catch small animals but it takes a lot of experience to do it well. The combination of built-in and learned behaviour is what gives them the skills they need to live.

Instinct and learning go together so naturally in behaviour that it's pretty hard to tell where one ends and the other begins.

Many instinctive behaviours are improved by experience and learning.

YOUNG WEAVERBIRD'S NEST

ANOTHER NEST BY THE SAME BIRD, YEARS LATER

BIRD SONGS ARE GREAT EXAMPLES OF INSTINCT AND LEARNING WORKING TOGETHER...

THEY'D BETTER BE...

AHEM! BIRDS SING TO ATTRACT MATES AND SCARE OFF INTRUDERS.

BIRDS OF THE SAME SPECIES MUST HAVE SIMILAR SONGS--OTHERWISE, HOW COULD ANYONE ELSE TELL WHAT KIND OF BIRD YOU WERE?

HEY, IT'S IMPORTANT IF YOU WANT A SOCIAL LIFE!

ALL SONGBIRDS HAVE A BUILT-IN ABILITY TO SING...

I WANT TO SINGGGGG !!!

...BUT IN DIFFERENT SONGBIRDS, THE ABILITY IS CHANGED IN DIFFERENT WAYS BY EXPERIENCE.

To learn and sing a normal chaffinch song, a young chaffinch must listen to and imitate other chaffinches.

HMMM...

CHAFFINCH

If the chaffinch is raised alone without songs to imitate, it will come up with an original song that sort of sounds like a chaffinch song — but not much.

WHAT ABOUT "♪"?

HMMM. OKAY.

SOUNDS PRETTY GOOD.

ALRIGHT. C-H-E-E -U-R-P.

If a group of young chaffinches is brought up together, the songs will be similar to each other but different from normal chaffinch songs.

SO CHAFFINCHES HAVE SOME PART OF THEIR SONG BUILT-IN, BUT HAVE TO LEARN MOST OF IT FROM OTHERS...

EXACTLY! BUT SOME SONGBIRDS DON'T HAVE TO LEARN FROM OLDER BIRDS...

HEY, NICE OUTFIT!

SONG SPARROW

Song sparrows raised alone end up singing perfect song-sparrow songs. But they do have to hear themselves practise to get it right.

Deaf song sparrows can't hear themselves sing, and end up with a very abnormal song.

SO A SONG SPARROW KNOWS HOW THE SONG SHOULD GO, BUT HAS TO PRACTISE TO GET IT, RIGHT?

THIS IS GREAT. CAN I KEEP IT?

YUP. IT'S A COMBINATION OF INSTINCT AND LEARNING.

OKAY, BUT ARE THERE ANY EXAMPLES THAT AREN'T SHRIEKING BIRDS?

HOW ABOUT SPITTING FISH?

SEEYA. IT'S TIME FOR MY WORLD TOUR...

PT!

ARCHER FISH

Archer fish shoot drops of water at insects nearby, knocking them off branches and into the water where the fish can eat them.

YOUNG ARCHER FISH HAVE THE INSTINCT TO SPIT, BUT THEIR AIM IS TERRIBLE!

ACK!

PT! PT! PT! PT! PT! PT! PT!

But as they grow, their aim improves with practice and the maturation of their spitting reflex. By the time they're adults, they can hit an insect on a branch one and a half metres away.

If you give a nut to a squirrel that has been raised without nuts, it will immediately try to gnaw it open.

19

BUT WHERE DO INSTINCTS COME FROM?

HOW DID LEARNING BEGIN?

HOW DID THIS STUFF FORM?

LET'S TAKE A LOOK!

HOW BEHAVIOUR DEVELOPS

Sowbugs live in dark, damp areas, like under rocks or in rotting logs. If you take some sowbugs and expose them to dry air or light, they'll start to wander around randomly.

SOWBUG

The drier the air is, the faster they move around. When they move into damper air they slow down, and if they get into a dark and moist place they'll stop. Sowbugs don't even have to think about moving — they just do it.

HOW 'BOUT ANOTHER EXAMPLE?

HOW 'BOUT GETTING TO THE POINT?

If a motmot is raised without parents, the bird will still have some of the built-in behaviours its parents have.

MOTMOT

Motmots mainly eat snakes. If you present a young motmot with a painted wooden stick, it will peck at it.

It will peck at any colour of painted stick...

...except one with yellow and red rings.

WHY NOT?

WELL, SOME OF THE SNAKES THAT LIVE IN THE AREA THE BIRDS DO ARE DEADLY CORAL SNAKES --SNAKES WITH RED AND YELLOW STRIPES.

SO HOW DID THIS BEHAVIOUR GET BUILT INTO THE BIRDS' BRAINS?

I'M GETTING TO IT!!

SHEESH, WHAT A GROUCH!

Every animal must do certain things to survive. For example, one of the most important things is eating.

AFTER ALL, IF YOU DON'T EAT, YOU'LL DIE.

Every animal has to eat, or else it won't grow up to be an adult and have babies.

YOU KNOW, EATING'S GREAT.

And since babies take after their parents, the babies that survive will want to eat too!

SURE IS!

BUT ANIMALS HAVE TO DO OTHER THINGS, TOO. TO STAY ALIVE, ANIMALS MUST:

WATCH FOR PREDATORS
RUN FROM PREDATORS
MAKE TERRITORIES
FIGHT OTHER ANIMALS
FIND MATES
ETC. ETC.

The better the animal is at any of these things, the better the chance it has of surviving to have babies — babies that act like it does.

If you're not as good at finding food...

I THINK I JUST DID SOMETHING VERY STUPID...

...or getting away from enemies...

...or thousands of other things, you're not likely to last long. Because of the forces of nature, some animals will survive to have babies, and some won't. This is called **natural selection**.

At the same time, every baby is different, and no baby is exactly the same as its parents. These differences are called **variation**.

Most of the differences don't do anything to help the animal survive any better.

But once in a while, you'll get a baby that can run a little faster, or hide better, or have some other slight advantage that will make it more likely to survive than others.

The most obvious wonders of evolution are in the *looks* of animals.

But what good are looks if the animal acts like an idiot?

STAY STILL YOU FOOL!

FOR ANY SPECIES TO SURVIVE BOTH ITS LOOKS **AND** ITS BEHAVIOUR MUST EVOLVE TO FIT ITS SURROUNDINGS.

AAAAAH!

TOLD YOU SO!

PLUCK!

SO WHAT ABOUT YOUR SOWBUGS?

WELL, SOWBUGS DON'T HAVE BIG BRAINS, BUT OVER THE YEARS THEY'VE EVOLVED A SIMPLE BEHAVIOUR THAT KEEPS THEM FROM DRYING OUT...

If it's dry or sunny, move around....

If it's damp and dark, stop.

Sowbugs that don't do that are more likely to dry out or to be eaten by birds — which won't help them survive to have baby sowbugs.

In the same way, motmot babies that go around pecking at poisonous snakes won't be having as many babies as motmots that avoid those snakes.

WHAT, ARE YOU NUTS?

THESE BABIES, IN TURN, ARE MORE LIKELY TO HAVE BABIES THAT ALSO AVOID DANGEROUS SNAKES...

...AND SO ON AND SO ON...

Behaviours are always slowly evolving to fit in with the animal's surroundings. Even closely-related species will develop different behaviours if it helps them survive better.

CAUTION
NEST CONSTRUCTION AREA

FOR EXAMPLE, MANY KINDS OF SEAGULLS MAKE THEIR NESTS ON THE GROUND, BUT...

...some types have chicks that are born camouflaged

and some have chicks that aren't.

Just after they've hatched, the gulls that have non-camouflaged chicks start to feed them...

...but parents of camouflaged babies ignore them at first. Instead they take time to pick up all of the white eggshell pieces and move them out of the nest.

WHAT'S GOING ON HERE?!

The non-camouflaged chicks are not disguised — they already stand out from the nest — so a few pieces of eggshell won't attract any extra attention from predators. The parents must protect them in other ways.

BACK OFF!

HEY!

On the other hand, camouflaged chicks hide quite nicely, but if the white eggshells are left in the nest they would give the chicks away. Parents who don't remove the shells are much more likely to lose their kids to predators.

Many more chicks whose parents moved shells would live to have chicks of their own, and eggshell-moving behaviour would become more common.

BUT THE BLACK-HEADED GULL'S BEHAVIOUR SEEMS THE WEIRDEST!

IT WAITS AN HOUR BEFORE MOVING EGGSHELLS!

WHY?

BLACK-HEADED GULL

DON'T EVEN THINK IT, BUSTER!

SLURP

For a very good reason: black-headed gulls will eat their neighbours' chicks when they're freshly hatched.

Strangely, once the chicks are dry, they won't be touched. It takes about an hour for a chick to dry after hatching.

STRANGELY, I'M NOT HUNGRY ANYMORE...

A black-headed gull parent has an extra predator to worry about for an hour so its behaviour must be different from that of its cousins.

27

For a species to continue, the animals in that species must mate. No one lives forever, and mating allows an animal to pass on its family traits.

For a male lion to father cubs, he must join a pride. And to join a pride, the lion must defeat the pride's current male and drive him away. Then he must kill all of the young cubs.

NOOOO! WHY?!

BECAUSE THE MOTHER WON'T MATE AGAIN UNTIL SHE HAS RAISED HER CUBS. SHE'LL STRUGGLE TO PROTECT THEM, BUT IF THEY'RE KILLED, SHE WILL MATE RIGHT AWAY...

And since a male lion only has a few years before another male tries to force *him* away, he can't afford to wait for someone else's cubs to grow up before he can have cubs of his own.

Of course, the lion doesn't think this all through. But as lions evolved over thousands of years, any lions that *did* wait for other guys' cubs to grow up first would have a much greater chance of never having cubs at all.

PLAN "A"

MAP

BREEDING STRATEGY!

THIS IS WHAT I GET FOR BEING NICE!

Over the years, this **"selfish"** behaviour became the way males behaved because selfish males ended up having most of the cubs. Most "unselfish" males had none.

SO AN ANIMAL'S BEHAVIOUR, WHETHER INSTINCTIVE OR LEARNED, IS SHAPED BY HOW ITS ANCESTORS EVOLVED.

Family Album

EVERYBODY NEEDS TO EAT AND DRINK, MATE, FLEE AND FIGHT, AND (SOMETIMES) RAISE THEIR YOUNG.

LET'S TAKE A CLOSER LOOK AT SOME OF THE IMPORTANT THINGS ANIMALS DO FOR A LIVING...

HEY, YOU CALL THE SHOTS, POP!

29

ANIMALS HAVE ALL SORTS OF WAYS OF MAKING SURE THEY GET FOOD AND WATER.

SLURP!

FEEDING

Many basic feeding behaviours are instinctive, which makes sense since finding food is so important. However, most animals can learn how to find food better as they grow up.

Chickadees instinctively know how to catch and hold grubs and worms with their feet.

CHICKADEE

Baby chickadees that are raised without being allowed to grab grubs can hold the food when they're given the chance.

OF COURSE, THEY DON'T HAVE MUCH STYLE, AT FIRST...

BUT WITH PRACTICE THEY GET AS GOOD AS NORMAL CHICKADEES.

CHIPS

Baby chicks peck at things by instinct, but they also watch their mother closely to see what is good to eat.

If a mother hen started pecking only, say, green seeds, the chick would start to peck only at green seeds.

WELL, MOM EATS THESE ONES, SO THEY MUST BE OKAY.

YAH COPYCAT!

As well as learning what it can eat, an animal must know what *not* to eat. Any farmer will tell you that rats are hard to kill with poison, because they're "bait-shy."

HMMM...

Rats are suspicious of anything new, so even if a scrumptious piece of food suddenly appears, a rat won't touch it for a few days.

When it does, it eats just a tiny nibble at first — only enough for the rat to get a little sick if the food is poisoned.

If the rat does get sick, it knows that the new food is bad and won't touch it ever again.

EVER?

EVER! RATS CAN'T THROW UP - THAT'S ONE WAY TO GET RID OF POISON - SO IF THEY DIDN'T WATCH WHAT THEY ATE, THEY COULD EASILY DIE!

AN ANIMAL'S TABLE MANNERS ARE AFFECTED BY HOW IT HAS TO GET FOOD.

BELLCH!

CRUNCH! GOBBLE! SMACK!

Wolves bolt their food down as fast as they can because they live and hunt in packs. When the group captures prey each wolf has to compete for a share of the meat. It must grab as much meat as it can before someone else takes it.

Lions, the only cats that live and hunt in groups, have this eating style too. So do dogs, showing the behaviour of their wolf-like ancestors.

CRUNCH! GOBBLE! SMACK!

On the other hand, most other cats, as well as foxes, hunt alone, so they don't have to worry about sharing food. They tend to take the food and hide it somewhere, coming back now and then to eat.

WHAT YOU EAT AFFECTS THE WAY YOU LIVE.

BURP!

Meat eaters need a big meal only once every few days because meat is loaded with nutrients.

...AND THAT'S ALL I NEED FOR A FEW MONTHS!

BUT PLANT EATERS MUST SPEND MOST OF THEIR TIME GRAZING TO GET THE NOURISHMENT THEY NEED. GRASS AND LEAVES AREN'T NEARLY AS NUTRITIOUS AS THE VEGETABLES HUMANS EAT.

CHEEZE OHS

JUMBO PACK

Harsh environments require special ways of feeding. Usually, animals living in deserts have bodies and organs that use water very efficiently. Some animals, like the kangaroo rat, get all the water they need from their food.

NEVER NEED TO DRINK... NOPE, NOT ME...

BUT SOMETIMES BEHAVIOUR ALONE CAN SOLVE THE PROBLEM. THE DESERT-LIVING DARKLING BEETLE HAS EVOLVED A BRILLIANT SOLUTION TO GET ITS WATER.

DARKLING BEETLE

The beetle buries itself in the sand overnight and cools down. When dawn comes, the beetle climbs out and tilts its body with its bottom in the air.

YAWN!

GURGLE GURGLE

SLURP
SLURP
SLURP

The morning dew hits the beetle and condenses into tiny water droplets on its cold shell. The droplets roll down and gather at its front end in a big, drinkable drop.

Humpback whales use bubbles to trap schools of fish. A whale blows a cloud of tiny bubbles below the fish. As the "bubble cloud" rises, the startled fish clump together in a nice, easy-to-eat group.

IS IT LEARNED OR INSTINCT?

AS USUAL IN MOST BIG-BRAINED MAMMALS, IT'S A MIX OF BOTH!

HUMPBACK WHALE

Whales, after all, naturally blow bubbles...

YOU CAN'T REALLY HELP IT WHEN YOU LIVE UNDERWATER.

LOOK AT THIS!

For two years, the young whales play and experiment with the bubbles, learning new tricks from each other. When they hit three years old, suddenly they're using bubble clouds to catch food.

COOL!

BY PLAYING WITH THEIR INSTINCTIVE BEHAVIOURS, THE YOUNG WHALES TEACH THEMSELVES TO FEED!

ONCE A WHALE LEARNS HOW TO FEED, IT DOESN'T CHANGE. ADULTS HARDLY EVER TRY NEW STYLES...

GROWN-UPS. WHAT CAN YOU DO?

35

Komodo dragons are huge lizards that live on a tropical island in Southeast Asia. They're big (up to ten feet long!) and heavy, and don't always bring down their prey — sometimes they'll just bite the animal and let it run off.

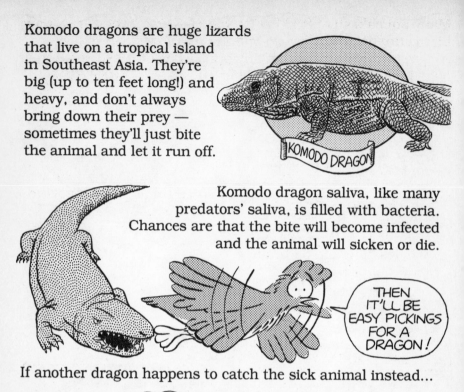

KOMODO DRAGON

Komodo dragon saliva, like many predators' saliva, is filled with bacteria. Chances are that the bite will become infected and the animal will sicken or die.

THEN IT'LL BE EASY PICKINGS FOR A DRAGON!

If another dragon happens to catch the sick animal instead...

...OH, WELL, MAYBE I'LL GET LUCKY TOMORROW

This behaviour "strategy" works on Komodo Island because dragons are the only predators.

IN MOST OTHER PLACES, THERE ARE SO MANY DIFFERENT PREDATORS THAT AN ANIMAL'S PREY WOULD PROBABLY GET EATEN BY AN ENTIRELY DIFFERENT SPECIES. SO MOST PREDATORS MUST KILL THEIR PREY RIGHT THEN AND THERE.

HMMM...YOU'RE LOOKING KIND OF QUEASY, KID... HOW ABOUT WE CHANGE THE TOPIC?

SURE...

NUTS

Many animals store food for the winter. These habits are always instinctive behaviours, since an animal that had to learn to store food might not survive its first winter.

OH NO! I FORGOT TO STORE NUTS!

THIS DOESN'T SEEM QUITE RIGHT, BUT I CAN'T PUT MY FINGER ON IT...

PAT PAT

Before the cold weather comes, squirrels start to push nuts into holes or cracks in trees. Squirrels raised indoors by people will try to hide nuts in holes or cracks in the wall or the corner of a room.

ACORN WOODPECKERS DRILL HUNDREDS OF HOLES IN TREES AND POLES TO FORM A NICE SET OF CUPBOARDS FOR HIDING ACORNS.

Birds and mammals that hide nuts often show amazing memory skills to remember where they hid their food.

Some birds can remember not only where their food is hidden, but also which spots have already been emptied.

ATE IT
STILL THERE
STILL THERE
STILL THERE
ATE IT
STILL THERE
ATE IT
ATE IT...

SOMETIMES DIFFERENT SPECIES TEAM UP THEIR BEHAVIOURS TO FIND FOOD...

The ratel (also known as the honey-badger) eats many things — eggs, small birds, fruits — but when it gets a chance it loves to eat honey and grubs.

RATEL

The African honeyguide loves to eat beeswax (it's even been known to eat beeswax candles!).

HONEYGUIDE

WHEN A HONEYGUIDE COMES UPON A RATEL, IT STARTS TO CHATTER AND JUMP AROUND EXCITEDLY!

The ratel hisses back, and they go into the forest together, the bird in front, chattering and leading the way.

When they get near a bee's nest (African bees live just about anywhere: in holes in trees, under rocks, or in the ground), the bird shuts up. The ratel finds the nest, tears it apart, and gorges on the honey and grubs. It's not hurt by bee stings...

WHAT A PIG!

38

When the ratel's finished, the honeyguide eats the wax and any leftover grubs.

BURP!

Honeyguides can't be learning this leading behaviour from their parents, because they never see them. The birds lay their eggs in other birds' nests to be raised. The honeyguide is programmed to do all this instinctively whenever it meets a ratel.

Scientists don't believe that honeyguides look for a ratel *after* finding a hive...

OKAY -- I'VE GOT A HIVE... NOW TO FIND A RATEL...

MAP

INSTEAD, THEY THINK THAT THE BIRD INSTINCTIVELY LEADS ANY RATEL IT MEETS DEEP INTO THE FOREST, WITH NO PARTICULAR DIRECTION IN MIND.

A RATEL! HOLY SMOKE! OOOOO! FOLLOW ME! FOLLOW ME!

Bees are pretty common, so it's never too long before the strange pair comes across a nest to raid.

THEY MAKE A NICE TEAM, BUT THE HONEYGUIDE AND THE RATEL DON'T NEED EACH OTHER; THEY DO EAT OTHER THINGS.

Kenya's dwarf mongoose and hornbill team is one of the very few cases where animals depend on each other a lot.

They both eat pretty much the same food — insects and small animals.

DWARF MONGOOSE

HORNBILL

Mongooses rarely look for food when the birds aren't around.

I HOPE THEY SHOW UP SOON! I'M GETTING HUNGRY!

The same goes for the hornbills — they even give the mongooses wake-up calls if they sleep in too long!

SQUAWK!

When the mongooses go hunting, they flush out enough prey for everybody.

BU WHA DO NA MONGOOFUS GED OWD UH VIT?

SAFETY. BY THEMSELVES, MONGOOSES HAVE TO CONSTANTLY KEEP WATCH FOR PREDATORS.

BRUSH BRUSH

BUT WORKING TOGETHER, THE HORNBILLS WATCH OUT FOR DANGER. SO THE MONGOOSES SPEND LESS TIME ON THE LOOKOUT AND MORE TIME HUNTING.

WELL, I'M DONE FEEDING.

ME TOO. FOREVER.

CHEEZE OHS

PRETZELS

DONUTS

40

DEFENCE

ALL ANIMALS HAVE BEHAVIOURS THAT HELP THEM TO AVOID DANGER WHENEVER THEY CAN.

YIPE!

One situation most baby mammals instinctively avoid is walking off cliffs.

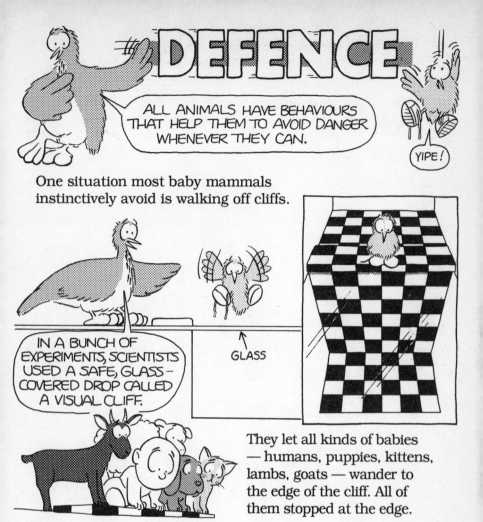

IN A BUNCH OF EXPERIMENTS, SCIENTISTS USED A SAFE, GLASS-COVERED DROP CALLED A VISUAL CLIFF.

GLASS

They let all kinds of babies — humans, puppies, kittens, lambs, goats — wander to the edge of the cliff. All of them stopped at the edge.

They could feel the glass across the gap, but their eyes told them that there was a dangerous drop.

If they were placed on the deep side, the babies would freeze or retreat to the "cliff" edge...

MEOW.

...except for the few mammals who use their sense of touch more than their eyes.

Other avoidance behaviours are less obvious. Young Nile crocodiles are usually active during the day and sleep at night. But African fish eagles started eating baby crocs along one part of the river.

BABY CROCODILE

Within days, the baby crocs in this area switched to being active at night and hiding during the day, when the eagles hunt. Babies that lived in eagle-free parts of the river kept to the day shift.

MAYBE I SHOULD CHANGE MY LIFESTYLE...

BUT YOU CAN'T ALWAYS AVOID DANGER...

RINGGGGGGGG

ZZZZ

...SOMETIMES YOU HAVE TO RUN FOR IT!

GLOOP!

For instance, if a shadow crosses an ocean fan-worm it will quickly pull into its tube.

Escape behaviour in birds, reptiles and mammals can be more complex. For instance, young ducks, chickens, and turkeys run from or ignore a shadow shape, depending on how it's coming toward them.

Moving one way, it looks like a hawk's shadow;

going the other way, it's more like a goose's.

For a while scientists thought that these responses were instinctive — a built-in defence against hawks. But now they think they're learned.

AT FIRST, CHICKS RUN FROM ANY SHADOW. OVER TIME, THEY LEARN THAT CERTAIN SHADOWS NEVER HURT THEM, SO THEY IGNORE THEM. BUT THEY STILL RUN FROM OTHER, UNFAMILIAR SHADOWS — LIKE A HAWK'S.

Some baby birds and mammals protect themselves by **imprinting** — following the first moving thing they see near them soon after they are born.

Usually that means Mom.

But some animals can imprint to almost anything: people, boots, cars, pieces of cloth, ultralight airplanes — though they imprint best to something that looks and sounds like their mother.

Once an animal has imprinted onto something, it follows it just like it would its mom. One famous animal-behaviour scientist often had ducklings imprinted to his boots.

The ducklings would follow him around in a line and quack at him as if he were an adult duck.

Baby goats imprint to their mother partly by sight, but mostly by smell.

MMMM... SMELLS LIKE MOM!

Baby shrews also imprint by smell. To get them where she wants them to go, a mother shrew rubs her babies against each other.

The sisters and brothers grab on to each other to form a "conga line," and Mom just leads the way!

CHA CHA CHA

SO WHAT'S THE USE OF IMPRINTING?

WELL, IT HELPS KEEP THE YOUNG CLOSE TO THEIR MOTHER...

CLACK!

This gives the young the best chance of escape. If a predator appears, the kids just go where Mom goes.

Staying in a close group behind Mom also makes the kids keep an eye on each other. This is important if you're going to live in groups for the rest of your life.

Many animals use plain old running to escape from attackers.

A rabbit heads for its burrow where it has an extra defence: if it's followed in, there are several tunnels inside to confuse any pursuers while the rabbit makes its escape out another hole.

Its cousin, the hare, uses a different strategy. When it sees a predator, it crouches and stops moving to hide itself. If the predator sees the hare and comes toward it, the hare will run.

But if it hasn't been spotted it will stay still unless the predator wanders too close. Then it will bolt, startling the attacker and giving the hare a head start.

Some insects show tricky action patterns that help them avoid becoming dinner for hungry bats.

TWO TYPES OF MOTHS HAVE EVOLVED A FLYING PATTERN THAT THEY USE WHEN THEY HEAR BAT CALLS (WHICH BATS USE TO FIND THEIR WAY AROUND AND LOCATE FOOD).

NOCTUID FAMILY

GEOMETRID FAMILY

If the moth hears a faint bat call — meaning that the bat is far away — it will instantly start to fly in a straight line away from the sound.

But if the calls are strong, the moth will suddenly flutter unpredictably.

Strong calls mean the bat is very near. The moth can't fly faster than the bat, but by flying this way, it makes itself much harder to catch.

THE MOTH ISN'T DOING A LOT OF FANCY THINKING ABOUT THE BAT...

...IT'S JUST REACTING TO THE SOUNDS THE BAT MAKES.

THE ONES THAT DON'T REACT MAKE AN EASIER MEAL FOR ME!

LACEWING

Another insect called a lacewing uses a different trick when it hears bat calls. When a lacewing hears that a bat is about half a metre away, it goes into a power dive.

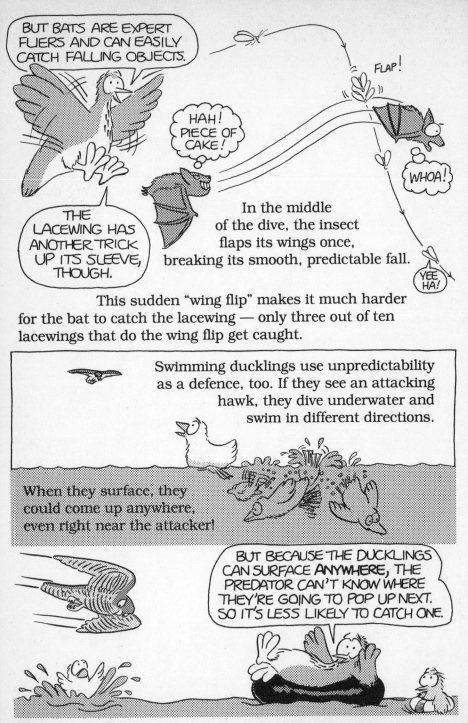

In the middle of the dive, the insect flaps its wings once, breaking its smooth, predictable fall.

This sudden "wing flip" makes it much harder for the bat to catch the lacewing — only three out of ten lacewings that do the wing flip get caught.

Swimming ducklings use unpredictability as a defence, too. If they see an attacking hawk, they dive underwater and swim in different directions.

When they surface, they could come up anywhere, even right near the attacker!

OH...I'M A GONER...I... COUGH...DIE... GASP...

One creative way some animals defend themselves is to act dead. When attacked, some birds, insects, snakes and mammals will go limp and hide all signs of life, hardly even breathing.

PLAYING DEAD ONLY WORKS IF THE OTHER ANIMAL ISN'T HUNGRY—JUST DEFENDING ITSELF —AND WILL GO AWAY IF THE THREAT IS GONE.

For example, a dog might attack a live snake, but would probably ignore a "dead" one.

Hognosed snakes and grass snakes both feign death nicely, with one little glitch. If threatened, the snake will flop over and lie there, with its mouth open and tongue hanging out.

LOOKS REAL TO ME!

THE PROBLEM IS THAT THIS INSTINCT TO FLIP OVER "DEAD" IS SO STRONG...

...THAT IF YOU TURN THE SNAKE THE RIGHT WAY UP...

FLIP!

...IT'LL FLOP OVER AGAIN! EVERY TIME!

FLOP!

OF COURSE, MOST ATTACKERS DON'T PLAY WITH THE DEAD SNAKE ENOUGH TO DISCOVER THIS...

49

Opossums have a much more polished act. When threatened or cornered, they threaten the attacker right back — growling, hissing, snapping and biting.

If that doesn't work, the opossum will suddenly drop "dead." It can be shaken or bitten without showing any signs of life.

OPOSSUMS ARE FULLY AWAKE DURING ALL OF THIS, BUT THEY DON'T REACT TO THE PAIN.

IT TAKES THEM SEVERAL MINUTES TO COME OUT OF THEIR LITTLE "TRANCE" AFTERWARD, TOO.

Playing dead can also be used as a last-ditch escape method. Some small birds will suddenly go limp when caught. A cat about to eat a dead bird will usually drop it on the ground to pluck it.

At that instant the jolt of being dropped may "wake up" the bird, giving it one last chance to escape.

OF COURSE, THIS TRICK DOESN'T ALWAYS WORK — CATS ARE VERY QUICK. BUT IT WORKS ENOUGH TO SAVE SOME BIRDS, WHO...

...PASS IT ON TO THEIR KIDS, BLAH, BLAH, BLAH.

ON THE OTHER HAND, IF THE BIRD KEEPS STRUGGLING THE CAT WILL ALMOST CERTAINLY BITE AND CLAW IT UNTIL IT'S DEAD.

But the award for best performance goes to...

THE WOOD SNAKE
of the West Indies

If attacked, it not only rolls over, but also releases a special chemical to make itself smell like it's already dead and rotting. It sends blood into its eyes, making them dull red, and bleeds from its mouth for that extra bit of realism.

THANK YOU... OH...THANK YOU SO MUCH... I'M AFRAID SHE CAN'T BE WITH US TONIGHT TO ACCEPT THIS AWARD...

CLAP!
CLAP!
CLAP!
CLAP!

One way some animals increase their chance of survival is by living in groups. There's strength in numbers.

Lions in a pride kill about twice as much per lion as lions who live and hunt alone.

GURGLE!

Birds in a flock are able to spend more time eating and less time looking out for danger than a bird on its own.

A solitary bird has to be constantly alert for danger. In a flock, it only occasionally has to watch out for enemies.

THE BEST SIZE FOR A GROUP BALANCES THE NEED FOR PROTECTION WITH THE NEED FOR FOOD...

For instance, if a flock is too small, each bird still spends a lot of its time looking out for danger, so it's got less eating time than it would if the flock were bigger.

If the group is too big, there's less lookout time and plenty of feeding time, but it's hard to find enough food to feed everybody.

Large groups are easier for predators to spot. Still, the bigger the group, the less likely it is that any one bird will be caught. It's easy to get lost in the crowd.

When a hawk attacks a flock of starlings, they fly off close together, zigzagging around each other. This makes it hard for the hawk to pick out one starling without colliding with other birds — not a safe thing to do in mid-air!

Colonies of black-headed gulls use
this safety in numbers to raise their chicks.
The birds all lay their eggs at about the same time.

IF THE EGGS WERE LAID AT DIFFERENT TIMES, PREDATORS COULD EAT EGGS AND CHICKS ALL THROUGH THE SEASON.

But they can only eat so many eggs a day before getting full. So if all of the eggs are out in the same week, not even the greediest predators can eat them all.

For the black-headed gulls, more eggs survive if everyone lays them at the same time.

Adélie penguins use the same strategy, and not only for laying eggs. Whenever they go into the water, they start by forming a large group on the shoreline.

ADÉLIE PENGUINS

They don't just hop in, because down below....

...wait penguin-eating leopard seals.

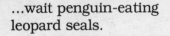

The bigger the group of penguins, the better any one penguin's chance of getting past the seals will be.

When you're trying to hide in the pack, the best place to be is somewhere in the middle.

FIRSTS AND LASTS STAND OUT MORE!

ANYWAY, THE WAITING PENGUINS START TO SHOVE AND JOSTLE EACH OTHER...

SPLOOSH!

...until someone falls in. Then the rest of them lean over to see what happens to it over the next few seconds. If it doesn't get eaten, everyone else quickly pours into the water.

WELL, SO MUCH FOR COOPERATION. THAT FIRST PENGUIN DIDN'T GET MUCH CHOICE!

BUT THAT'S AN IMPORTANT POINT. ANIMALS DON'T LIVE IN GROUPS JUST TO BE NICE. THEY DO IT TO HELP THEMSELVES.

THEY'RE *SELFISH*?!

YES, THEY'RE PROTECTING THEMSELVES.

HERDS AND FLOCKS STAY TOGETHER BECAUSE GETTING SEPARATED MAKES YOU STICK OUT. AND IF YOU STICK OUT, YOU'RE MORE LIKELY TO GET EATEN.

But that doesn't mean animals in groups don't cooperate. Groups can have some pretty complicated defences. When a muskox herd is attacked by wolves, the whole herd goes into a defensive formation that protects everybody.

MUSKOX

IF THEY'RE SURROUNDED, THEY FORM A CIRCLE WITH THE CALVES IN THE CENTRE. THEN BULLS AND COWS WILL, ONE AT A TIME, CHARGE OUT AT THE WOLVES.

If the wolves don't find any weak animals, they'll give up after a little while.
The muskoxen could keep it up all day.

Even with this kind of cooperation, the animals that do best in herds and groups are the young and healthy ones. When attacking a group, predators usually try to separate out one animal.

THE OLD OR SICK WILL BE SLOWER AND MORE LIKELY TO STAND OUT.

But sometimes — very rarely — the tables are turned on the predator. **Mobbing** is a surprising behaviour, in which prey animals surround and attack an animal that usually hunts them.

GREAT HORNED OWL

A typical mobbing situation starts when a bird of prey has been sitting near the territories of prey birds. Quite suddenly, some of those birds will surround it.

56

The little birds dart and jump around with quick, twitchy motions, calling and screeching. They attack the owl by clawing at its head and neck, or diving at it and veering away at the last moment. Nearby birds hear the commotion and join in. Even tiny hummingbirds take part, trying to jab at the owl's eyes.

Eventually, the nervous owl will fly away, often getting chased for a bit.

IT TAKES QUITE A WHILE FOR THE ATTACKING BIRDS TO CALM DOWN, TOO!

Seabirds will mob threatening birds or mammals (like humans) that get too close to a colony.

Mammals also mob. Meerkats (small, timid cousins of the mongoose) usually run from large snakes that could eat them.

But if several meerkats are confronted by a snake, they surround and attack it, driving it away from their territories.

NORMALLY, MANY OF THESE ANIMALS HAVE A BUILT-IN ACTION PATTERN TO AVOID DANGER.

BUT AT A TIME OF MOBBING, THEY QUICKLY JOIN IN.

EEP!

MOB. I MUST MOB.

EVEN THOUGH IT SEEMS SORT OF NUTS, MOBBING DOES HELP THE ANIMALS AND THEIR FAMILIES TO SURVIVE.

AN ENEMY WHO'S BEEN MOBBED WON'T GO NEAR THAT AREA AGAIN.

BOY, THAT GAVE ME THE WILLIES!

THAT'S ONE LESS OWL TO WORRY ABOUT!

HEE-YA! IT'S LIKE SMALL ANIMAL SELF-DEFENCE!

MEERKAT

ANOTHER WAY GROUPS CAN DEFEND THEMSELVES IS BY MAKING NOISE TO WARN OTHERS OF PREDATORS!

Beavers slap their tails on water, making a loud smack to alert their denmates.

Many birds cry out when a predator approaches, alerting other birds around them.

WAIT A MINUTE! ISN'T THE NOISY ALARM CALLER GETTING INTO MORE TROUBLE BY ATTRACTING ATTENTION?!

THAT'S A BIG PROBLEM, AND THERE ARE DIFFERENT WAYS AROUND IT.

The beaver's tail alarm is quick and loud, meant to startle any animal nearby.

SMACK!

Immediately after slapping, the beaver dives underwater to make its getaway.

Bird alarms, by contrast, are often long and low, slowly fading away after a few seconds.

WEEEEEEEEAAAAAAAAAaaa

This makes it hard to tell exactly what direction the sound is coming from.

PIGEONS HAVE A DIFFERENT ALARM SYSTEM. NORMALLY, A PIGEON MAKES A FEW BOBBING MOVEMENTS BEFORE IT FLIES OFF.

WHOA, BOY, WHOA!

PIGEON

This signals to the pigeons around it that it's getting ready to fly...

But when a pigeon spots danger coming, it takes off without bobbing. This alerts nearby pigeons, and they fly off too. The explosion of flying pigeons helps to confuse the attacker.

UH-OH, TROUBLE

Confusion also works with alarm calls. If a Belding's ground squirrel sees an attacker like a hawk or a falcon in the air, the squirrel gives an alarm whistle and heads to a burrow.

BELDING'S GROUND SQUIRREL

As everyone runs for cover, there's a mad, confusing scramble.

THE ALARM GIVER IS SAFER THAN IT WOULD BE JUST RUNNING AWAY BECAUSE IT CAN HIDE IN THE SCRAMBLING CROWD.

BUT HOW ABOUT SOME WEIRDER ALARM CALLS?

One strange alarm call is the cry a rabbit makes when it's caught. It suddenly lets out a long, loud scream that can be heard a long way away.

AAAAAAAAAAAHHHH!

IT'S NOT A QUICK, SHARP CRY TO STARTLE THE ATTACKER, AND OTHER RABBITS IGNORE THE CRY.

Scientists think that the cry is a last-ditch attempt to attract any other predators that might be nearby, who could create a disturbance or fight. This could give the rabbit a chance to get away.

HEY, WATCHA GOT THERE?

MIND YOUR OWN BUSINESS!

THIS TRICK WOULDN'T WORK TOO OFTEN, BUT WHAT HAS THE RABBIT GOT TO LOSE?

One last strange defence behaviour is found in the Thompson's gazelle: it's called **stotting** or **pronking**. When the gazelle is approached by an enemy, it pops high in the air from all four legs, and flashes its white tail.

"STOTTING"? "PRONKING"? HOW ABOUT A MORE DIGNIFIED NAME?

HOW ABOUT A MORE DIGNIFIED BEHAVIOUR?

This sort of behaviour could be a signal for all sorts of things. But it's very hard to tell what this one is for.

POINK POINK

FLEEING
WARNING FAMILY
WARNING OTHE...

After stotting the gazelle may run or it may continue grazing.

POINK POINK

FLEEING
WARNING FAMILY
WARN... OT...

SO IT ISN'T USED FOR ESCAPE...

FLEEING
WARNING FAMILY
WARNING OT...

POINK

It stots whether it's in a herd or not — even when there are no other gazelles to be seen.

It will stot before a chase or after it has escaped from a chase...

POINK POINK POINK

SO WHAT'S IT FOR?!

...G POINK
WAR...NING FAMIL...
WARNIN... ...ERS

It seems that stotting sends a message to the *predator*, that it has been noticed.

Predators usually depend on surprise attacks. When a gazelle knows the attacker is near, it's much more likely to be able to escape. Certainly, it will make the predator run for its meal. Often, after seeing a gazelle stot, a leopard will just give up and wait for an easier meal.

It's a weird behaviour, but it does help both animals. If the leopard knows that it's been noticed, it probably won't waste its time and energy chasing a dinner that might get away.

And by giving the signal, the gazelle may prevent a chase and give itself more time to graze.

CLEANING

OR FEATHERS!

Animals stay healthy by making sure their skin and fur are clean and have no parasites. But some cleaning behaviors don't look so clean at first.

Pigs and rhinos love to soak in mud or roll in dust, getting a nice coating of dirt.

THIS LOOKS FILTHY, BUT IT ACTUALLY DOES HAVE A CLEANING EFFECT:

MUD
GLUB
SKIN

MUD
SKIN

THE MUD COVERS AND KILLS PARASITES ON THE SKIN...

...AND MAKES A LAYER THAT NEW BUGS CAN'T GET THROUGH TO BITE OR LAY EGGS.

IT ALSO HELPS REMOVE DEAD SKIN...

...KEEPS YOU COOL, AND ACTS LIKE A SUNSCREEN.

BUT MUD ISN'T THE ONLY WAY TO KEEP CLEAN. MANY ANIMALS SPEND A LOT OF TIME GROOMING THEIR FUR OR FEATHERS.

Flies and bees lick and comb off dirt and pollen to get rid of extra weight and keep all systems "go."

Most small mammals lick, nibble or scratch at their fur.

A rat's routine is an action pattern. Even rats with no front paws go through the same motions, though they don't do anything.

Birds preen (comb their beaks through their feathers).

Most birds also waterproof their feathers with oil from a gland near their tails.

For those hard-to-reach spots, apes and monkeys groom each other, combing through fur to pick out bugs....

BUT WHAT IF MOST OF YOUR BODY'S A HARD-TO-REACH SPOT?

THEN YOU MAY NEED A LITTLE MORE HELP!

SCRITCH SCRITCH

Many types of small fish and shrimps are cleaners for bigger fish. The cleaners get all of their food by busily nibbling off parasites and infection.

Sometimes there are even long line-ups of customers waiting to be cleaned!

TAKE A NUMBER
27

SHE'S IN HIS MOUTH! DON'T THEY GET EATEN?

HARDLY EVER. BIG FISH DO EAT OTHER SMALL FISH, BUT THEY AVOID EATING CLEANERS.

WITHOUT THEM EVERYBODY WOULD GET SICK PRETTY QUICKLY.

On land, certain birds fill the same need for large hoofed mammals, by eating the bugs the mammals attract.

FOR A PRICE, THE OXPECKER PULLS HAIR FROM THE ANIMAL FOR ITS NEST.

OW. BUT IT'S WORTH IT.

A bird will stick with its ride for years, even making alarm calls if it sees danger coming. If the animal doesn't run, the bird will panic — to protect its meal ticket!

MOVE IT, FATSO! IT'S HARD TO FIND ANOTHER UNOCCUPIED PIG!

A few birds, like the Egyptian plover, clean around crocodiles, and will even go inside their mouths to pick at their gums!

ACTUALLY, IT'S NOT AS DANGEROUS AS IT LOOKS. WHEN CROCS BASK IN THE SUN, THEY IGNORE ALMOST EVERYTHING...

EGYPTIAN PLOVER

GREAT, THEN YOU CAN TRY IT. ANY OTHER WEIRD RELATIVES I SHOULD KNOW ABOUT?

HOW'S THIS FOR WEIRD?

Crows and jays have been known to perform bizarre behaviours called **smoke-bathing** and **anting**.

In anting, a bird sits on an ant colony and lets the insects run all over it. To defend the nest, the ants spray an acid on the intruder.

To smoke-bathe, a bird ruffles and spreads its feathers over a smouldering fire or a chimney and lets the smoke flow through.

THE BIRD WILL EVEN PICK UP ANTS AND WIPE THEM THROUGH ITS FEATHERS.

SOME BIRDS HAVE EVEN TRIED TO BATHE IN FLAMES!

No one is sure exactly why they do this, but it's thought that the smoke and acid help kill skin parasites on the bird.

TAP TAP

MAYBE THEY'RE JUST A FEW FEATHERS SHORT OF A DUSTER!

IN MOST GROUPS OF ANIMALS, THERE'S COMPETITION FOR FOOD, TERRITORY OR MATES. OFTEN, THE RESULT IS:
STOMP
FIGHTING
NOW THAT WE'RE CLEAN, TIME TO GET DIRTY AGAIN!

Fighting with another animal of your own species is different from fighting with a predator or prey animal.

WHAT A WASTE...

It doesn't help an animal (or its species) if both fighters get hurt or killed — it means two animals have destroyed themselves without having kids.

I'LL BEAT YOU NEXT YEAR!

Over the generations, animals that fought to the death wouldn't have as many babies as those with a built-in behaviour to quit before things got really nasty.

In a fight, even if no one gets killed, both winner and loser can get injured. Even small wounds can cause health problems. Another competitor can then easily polish off the winner.

HEY, EVERYBODY! I WON! HEY! HELLO?

RUMBLE RUMBLE

WHAP!

WHEN THEY'RE DEFENDING THEMSELVES AGAINST LIONS, GIRAFFES USE SWIFT KICKS WITH THEIR SHARP HOOVES.

BUT WHEN THEY'RE FIGHTING EACH OTHER, THEY "NECK" – IT NEEDS LOTS OF STRENGTH, BUT IT'S NOT VERY DANGEROUS.

Rattlesnakes never use their sharp, venom-filled fangs when they fight each other for mates (rattlesnakes that did that would have killed each other off long ago). So when they compete, they push each other.

Most antelopes, deer, and gazelles have sharp horns or antlers, but only fight each other by locking horns and pushing. Some even have ridgey horns for extra grip.

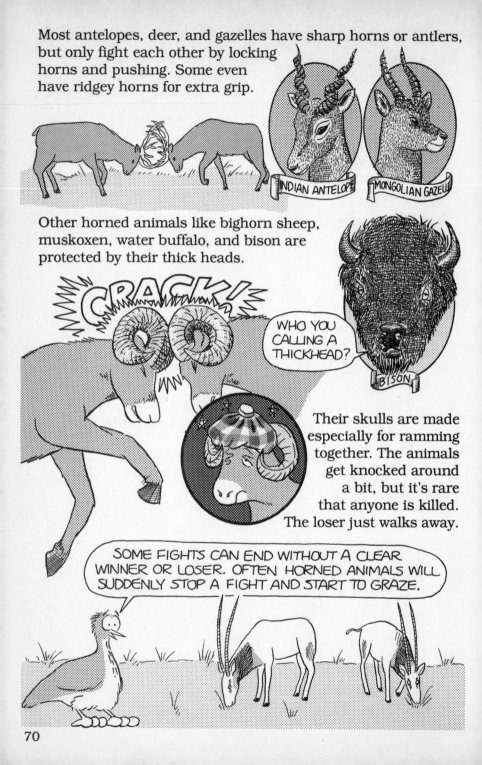

INDIAN ANTELOPE

MONGOLIAN GAZELLE

Other horned animals like bighorn sheep, muskoxen, water buffalo, and bison are protected by their thick heads.

CRACK!

WHO YOU CALLING A THICKHEAD?

BISON

Their skulls are made especially for ramming together. The animals get knocked around a bit, but it's rare that anyone is killed. The loser just walks away.

SOME FIGHTS CAN END WITHOUT A CLEAR WINNER OR LOSER. OFTEN, HORNED ANIMALS WILL SUDDENLY STOP A FIGHT AND START TO GRAZE.

This doesn't mean that some animal fights don't get violent.

Fighting walruses can give each other huge bloody gashes with their tusks.

A few moose die each year from fight wounds.

Rocky mountain goat fights are often vicious, and can end with one or both fighters badly injured or dead.

THEY DON'T BUTT HEADS; THEY STAB AT EACH OTHER WITH THEIR SHORT, SHARP HORNS.

Some animals try to avoid fighting altogether. When toads call for mates, their croaks range in pitch depending on their sizes (the lower the croak, the bigger the toad).

PEEP PEEP

BRAAAAA

The small toad gets the hint not to bother tackling the big toad.

Red deer stage roaring contests to see who can roar the longest. The larger, stronger deer always wins.

It saves everyone energy if no one has to fight.

ROOOOAAAAR

ROOOAACK COUGH COUGH HACK COUGH

One way that animals in a group can avoid fighting each other is to figure out who's the strongest. This dominant animal heads up the group.

The head male is the one who decides where the pack goes and when.

The top hyena in any clan is always female. She gets the best food of any clan member. Her daughter, if she survives, will become leader.

Many animals fall into a "pecking order," where the #1 animal can boss around everyone else, #2 can boss around everyone except #1, and so on....

This cuts down on a lot of group squabbling.

SINCE EVERYONE HAS THEIR OWN PLACE IN THE PECKING ORDER, THE LOWER ONES DON'T EVEN TRY TO TAKE ON THE HIGHER ONES.

BUT DON'T THEY HAVE TO FIGHT TO DECIDE WHO'S ON TOP?

YES, BUT ONCE THAT'S DONE WITH, THINGS SETTLE DOWN.

So when two animals meet, instead of fighting to find out where they stand with each other, the lower-ranked animal will bow to the higher-ranked one and everyone goes away satisfied.

Another way to avoid fighting others of your own kind is to make territories. In the wild, most animals learn to avoid others' territories so as not to run into each other.

TERRITORY OF
Mr R. W. BLACKBIRD
NO TRESPASSING
THIS MEANS YOU!

Since they don't see each other as much, they don't fight and get hurt as much, either.

Moose are very territorial during mating season, and avoid everybody but potential mates. Other animals, like bears, are loners all year round.

...HOPE SHE DOESN'T SEE ME LIKE THIS...

To establish a territory, most animals mark it out as their own.

WOLVES SCENT-MARK THEIR TERRITORY'S BOUNDARIES BY PEEING ON LANDMARKS LIKE TREES AND SHRUBS.

...AND WE ALL KNOW WHO ELSE DOES THIS WHEN TAKE THEM FOR WALKS, DON'T WE?

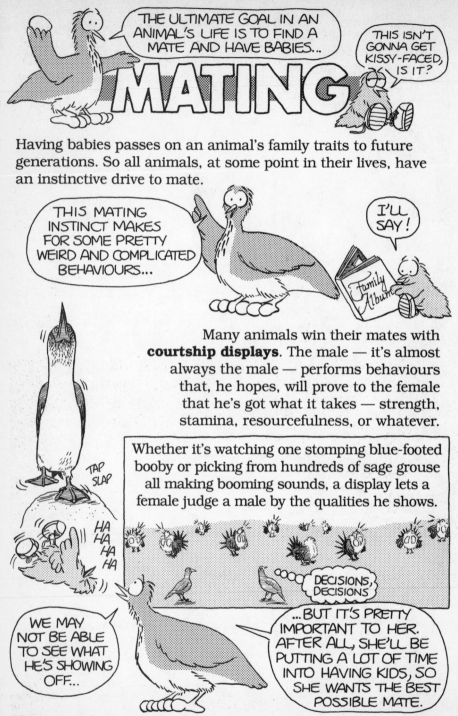

THE ULTIMATE GOAL IN AN ANIMAL'S LIFE IS TO FIND A MATE AND HAVE BABIES...

THIS ISN'T GONNA GET KISSY-FACED, IS IT?

MATING

Having babies passes on an animal's family traits to future generations. So all animals, at some point in their lives, have an instinctive drive to mate.

THIS MATING INSTINCT MAKES FOR SOME PRETTY WEIRD AND COMPLICATED BEHAVIOURS...

I'LL SAY!

Family Album

Many animals win their mates with **courtship displays**. The male — it's almost always the male — performs behaviours that, he hopes, will prove to the female that he's got what it takes — strength, stamina, resourcefulness, or whatever.

TAP SLAP

HA HA HA HA

Whether it's watching one stomping blue-footed booby or picking from hundreds of sage grouse all making booming sounds, a display lets a female judge a male by the qualities he shows.

DECISIONS, DECISIONS

WE MAY NOT BE ABLE TO SEE WHAT HE'S SHOWING OFF...

...BUT IT'S PRETTY IMPORTANT TO HER. AFTER ALL, SHE'LL BE PUTTING A LOT OF TIME INTO HAVING KIDS, SO SHE WANTS THE BEST POSSIBLE MATE.

Animals' courtship displays have several other functions:

1. To help them find each other.

Since males and females don't hang around together, sending out signals will make them more noticeable. Some female moths send out scent signals that travel for kilometres.

OOH!

2. To help sort out what species they are.

Bird songs and displays are different for every species.

Fireflies blink their lights in different patterns at different rates, depending on their species and sex.

NOPE,

HEY! NICE BLINK!

THIS HELPS MAKE SURE THAT ANIMALS DON'T WASTE TIME AND ENERGY TRYING TO MATE WITH THE WRONG KIND OF ANIMAL!

SPOOKY!

3. Once the right pair find each other, displays help make both of them willing to mate.

Courtship displays aren't always straightforward. Often it looks as if the animal can't decide what to do.

THREE-SPINED STICKLEBACK

A male three-spined stickleback builds a nest and guards it fiercely from strangers.

If a female approaches, he charges her like an enemy until he sees...

...she's a female bulging with eggs. He swims toward his nest to guide her.

But when he turns around, he charges her again until he sees her belly. Then he starts to guide her again.

He ends up doing a weird zigzag dance.

MAKE UP YOUR MIND!

As they get closer to the nest, his guiding instincts take over and he lets her into the nest to lay her eggs.

RUMBLE RUMBLE RUMBLE RUMBLE RUMBLE RUMBLE RUMBLE RUMBLE RUMBLE RUMBLE RUMBLE RUMBLE

RHINO COURTING IS PRETTY TOUGH!

FOR HOURS BEFORE MATING, THE TWO RHINOS SLUG IT OUT...

YIPE!

Neither gets seriously hurt, but they do get cut and bruised. For many years, worried zookeepers would break up the fights — and wonder why they weren't getting any baby rhinos.

78

BIRDS HAVE VERY SHOWY COURTSHIP DISPLAYS.

OFTEN THE MALE DANCES OR STRUTS IN FRONT OF THE FEMALE, SPREADING HIS FEATHERS AND LOOKING IMPRESSIVE.

WANDERING ALBATROSS

If the female approves of the male, she will often join his dance. They may perform a series of ritual movements before they mate.

PEER PRESSURE.

The male yellow-shafted flicker prepares for courtship by guarding his territory and singing loudly.

W-SHAFTED FLICKER

He will attack any male...

@*#!

...but not females!

Over time, one female visits more often than the others, and they start to build a nest together. The male dances for her...

...then attacks and chases her!

But the attack is only a part of his courtship display, and it helps make her more agreeable to mating.

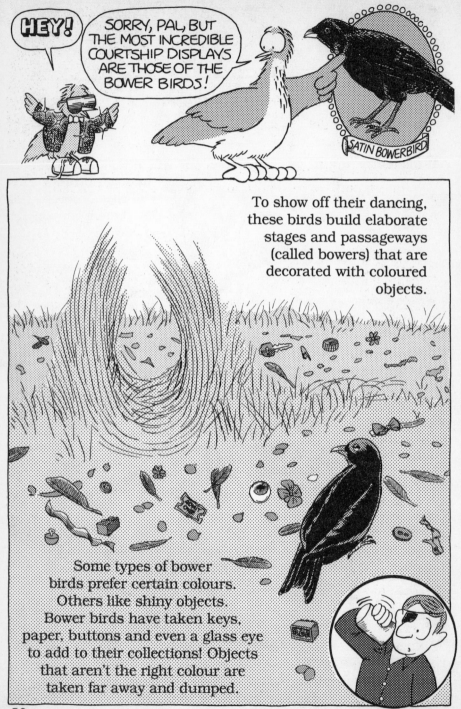

HEY!

SORRY, PAL, BUT
THE MOST INCREDIBLE
COURTSHIP DISPLAYS
ARE THOSE OF THE
BOWER BIRDS!

SATIN BOWERBIRD

To show off their dancing,
these birds build elaborate
stages and passageways
(called bowers) that are
decorated with coloured
objects.

Some types of bower
birds prefer certain colours.
Others like shiny objects.
Bower birds have taken keys,
paper, buttons and even a glass eye
to add to their collections! Objects
that aren't the right colour are
taken far away and dumped.

Some bower birds even mix their saliva with fruit juice or charcoal and paint it on the inside of the bower, using a stick as a paintbrush!

When a female enters the bower, the male struts and dances, holding up parts of his collection to show off. She probably mates with the male with the flashiest collection.

YOU REALLY HAVE BIRDS ON THE BRAIN, DON'T YA?

HEY, BIRDS HAVE THE FLASHIEST DISPLAYS. MOST OTHER ANIMALS AREN'T AS SHOWY.

Displaying is just one way of getting a mate. Many mammals, of course, fight each other for mates. The winners of these battles go on to mate and have the babies.

But some mammals do display. A male hedgehog walks in circles around a female for hours, snuffling and snorting constantly....

SNORT
SNUFFLE
OINK
SNORT
SNORF

APPARENTLY FEMALE HEDGEHOGS FIND THIS ATTRACTIVE.

THEY DON'T GET OUT MUCH, DO THEY?

Like birds, many fish have colourful and complex courtships, too!

As mating season comes along, many of them start to advertise, changing colour (and personality!) to try to get a mate.

MILD-MANNERED MALE CUCKOO WRASSE ELEVEN MONTHS OF THE YEAR

HEY BABY!

HOT-TO-TROT MALE CUCKOO WRASSE ONE MONTH OF THE YEAR

But displaying is also dangerous, because any flashy show meant to attract mates can also attract predators.

SOMETIMES IT'S A TOSS-UP WHETHER THE ANIMAL GETS A MATE OR GETS EATEN!

OH DARLING! COME 'N' GET ME!

IF YOU INSIST...

Tungara frogs call loudly for hours to attract female frogs.

WHINE-CHUCK!

WHINE-CHUCK!

WHINE-YAAAA!

But their loud croaks also make it easy for fringe-lipped bats to find them.

Some animals fake mating calls to attract a meal....

Predator fireflies can imitate other species, flashing their lights in the same patterns.

HI LOVERBOY!

When a lovelorn firefly shows up, expecting a mate, the faker eats him.

SO THAT'S THE BASICS OF MATING!

SO WHAT'S NEXT?

YOU KNOW. FIRST COMES LOVE, THEN COMES MARRIAGE, THEN COMES MR. AND MRS. RHINO WITH THE BABY CARRIAGE...

ANIMALS USUALLY PUT A LOT OF EFFORT INTO TAKING CARE OF THEIR LITTLE BUNDLES OF JOY.

WHOA!

UH-OH

YOU DON'T, POP!

NO, BUT MANY CREATURES GET PRETTY TESTY IF YOU GO NEAR THEIR BABIES...

PARENTING

Of course, this isn't true of species that don't look after their young. Many animals, like sea turtles, lay their eggs in a safe spot and hope for the best.

YOU'RE ON YOUR OWN, KIDDIES...

OH NO, HE'S GOT RAPHAEL!

Usually in these cases many eggs are laid, because most of the unprotected young will be lost to predators.

OTHER PARENTS LEAVE A GIFT -- SOME FOOD FOR THE NEWLY-HATCHED BABY. DUNG BEETLES LAY AN EGG ON A BIG, TASTY BALL OF DUNG.

CHOMP!

MMM! MOM AND DAD SURE MUST'VE LOVED ME!

But the young of many other animals (including most birds and mammals) aren't ready to go out on their own right away. So their parents have instinctive behaviours to take care of them as they grow.

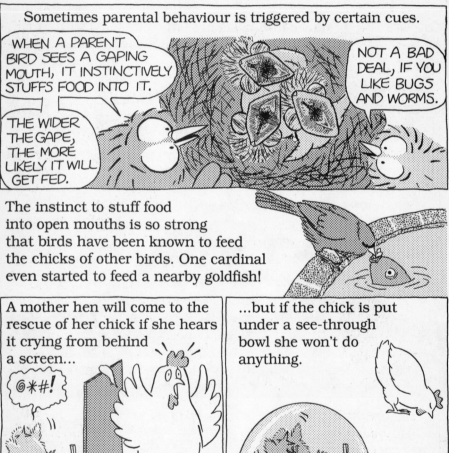

Sometimes parental behaviour is triggered by certain cues.

WHEN A PARENT BIRD SEES A GAPING MOUTH, IT INSTINCTIVELY STUFFS FOOD INTO IT.

THE WIDER THE GAPE, THE MORE LIKELY IT WILL GET FED.

NOT A BAD DEAL, IF YOU LIKE BUGS AND WORMS.

The instinct to stuff food into open mouths is so strong that birds have been known to feed the chicks of other birds. One cardinal even started to feed a nearby goldfish!

A mother hen will come to the rescue of her chick if she hears it crying from behind a screen...

@*#!

...but if the chick is put under a see-through bowl she won't do anything.

She can see the chick yelling, but she can't hear it. Only the sound of the chick triggers her "mothering" behaviour.

Some parenting instincts are so strong that an adult will even take care of young that it isn't related to.

WOLVES REGURGITATE FOOD FOR CUBS IN THEIR PACK. IT'S EASY TO CARRY, AND EASY FOR THE KIDS TO DIGEST.

THE THING IS, IF YOU PUT A CUB IN FRONT OF A TAME WOLF THAT'S BEEN RAISED BY HUMANS, IT WILL SUDDENLY BARF UP FOOD FOR THE CUB.

CHARMING.

A nesting sooty tern will peck at any animal that approaches its nest, including stray baby tern chicks.

G'WAN! SCRAM!

SOOTY TERN

But if the chick manages to dodge the adult's beak and touch her chest, the adult will stop pecking and will act like a mother to the new chick.

Stranger still, if the chick *does* get driven off and another tern pecks at it, its cries will make the *first* adult rush to help it!

SHRIEK!!

I'LL SAVE YOU!!

WELL, I'M CONFUSED!

BOY, THESE BIRD INSTINCTS SEEM SORT OF ROBOT-LIKE, DON'T THEY?

YOU WANT ROBOT-LIKE? MOST BIRDS ARE "PROGRAMMED" BY INSTINCT TO ONLY PAY ATTENTION TO WHAT'S IN THEIR NEST, AND IGNORE ANYTHING OUTSIDE OF IT.

If a chick falls out of the nest, tough luck! The parents won't notice it or its cries and it will eventually die.

There are some birds that take advantage of these rigid behaviours.

EURASIAN CUCKOO

Cuckoos don't bother sitting on their eggs. Instead they lay their eggs in other birds' nests so that the other birds can hatch and raise them.

ON TO THE NEXT NEST!

CUCKOO EGG

When the cuckoo chick hatches, it's bigger, stronger and makes more noise than the other babies. This attracts more attention, so it gets fed more often than the others.

ME!

ME!

ME!

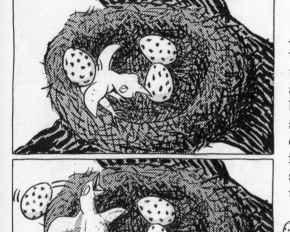

As if this isn't enough, when the cuckoo's about ten hours old it develops a nasty reflex. When its back is touched by something — usually other eggs or chicks — it starts pushing and shoving the object until it's heaved over the side of the nest.

YIKES!

After about two weeks, the cuckoo is alone in the nest and the shoving reflex disappears.

The parent ignores its own dying chicks outside the nest and continues to feed the cuckoo — sometimes until the young bird is a lot bigger than the parent.

MY SIDE OF THE FAMILY, OBVIOUSLY...

BUT MANY TYPES OF BIRDS THAT ARE VICTIMS OF CUCKOOS HAVE EVOLVED WAYS OF WATCHING OUT FOR THEIR EGGS. IF A BIRD THINKS AN EGG IS SUSPICIOUS, IT MAY:

Push the suspicious egg out.

Build over the egg.

Abandon the nest.

These birds spot suspicious eggs by looking out for one that's different. Scientists figured this out when they replaced all but one egg in some bird nests with different ones. The birds pushed out the non-matching egg — their own.

OF COURSE, THIS NEVER HAPPENS IN THE WILD, BECAUSE CUCKOOS LAY ONLY ONE EGG PER NEST.

OTHERWISE, THE CUCKOO CHICKS WOULD TRY TO KILL EACH OTHER!

Many ground-nesting birds perform a built-in behaviour called a **distraction display** when a threat is near.

PREDATORS OFTEN MISS THE WELL-CAMOUFLAGED BIRDS AND THEIR NESTS.

But if the threat gets too close, the parent will suddenly fly from the nest...

...then flutter limply to the ground several metres away.

It ruffles its feathers to look like a sick bird, and hops around dragging one or both wings as if they were broken. The bird might even flop to the ground as if it were exhausted.

All of this is pretty hard for the predator not to notice.

But as the attacker approaches the "wounded" prey, the bird will slowly drag itself along — always at a safe distance — leading the predator away from the nest.

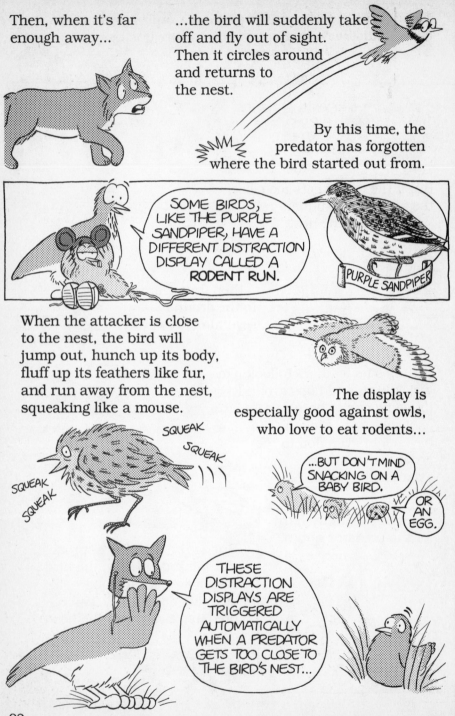

Then, when it's far enough away...

...the bird will suddenly take off and fly out of sight. Then it circles around and returns to the nest.

By this time, the predator has forgotten where the bird started out from.

SOME BIRDS, LIKE THE PURPLE SANDPIPER, HAVE A DIFFERENT DISTRACTION DISPLAY CALLED A **RODENT RUN.**

PURPLE SANDPIPER

When the attacker is close to the nest, the bird will jump out, hunch up its body, fluff up its feathers like fur, and run away from the nest, squeaking like a mouse.

The display is especially good against owls, who love to eat rodents...

SQUEAK
SQUEAK
SQUEAK
SQUEAK

...BUT DON'T MIND SNACKING ON A BABY BIRD.

OR AN EGG.

THESE DISTRACTION DISPLAYS ARE TRIGGERED AUTOMATICALLY WHEN A PREDATOR GETS TOO CLOSE TO THE BIRD'S NEST...

PARENTING ISN'T ALL INSTINCT -- THERE'S LEARNING INVOLVED TOO. MANY ANIMALS HAVE SOME INSTINCTIVE IDEA OF HOW TO RAISE THEIR YOUNG, BUT DO A BETTER JOB WITH LATER BABIES...

SCRITCH SCRITCH

One Mexican trogon was seen catching insects for his babies. But once he got home he didn't seem to know what to do with the food. So he just stood there in front of the peeping chicks. (Later on, he did learn to feed the chicks properly.)

Sometimes parental instincts actually keep the parent from helping the young.

After being born, a kangaroo pup is raised in its mother's pouch.

...but to get into the pouch, it's got to crawl there first!

RED KANGAROO

POUCH OPENING
X

...AND THAT'S NOT EASY WHEN YOU'RE BLIND AND THE SIZE OF A PAPER CLIP!

94

Some pups lose their way and die, but the mother doesn't help the newborn at all; it must make it on its own. This may ensure that the pup is healthy and in good working order.

Once the pup is in the pouch, though, it's a different story....

THE JOEY IS VERY WELL CARED FOR AS IT SPENDS THE NEXT EIGHT MONTHS LIVING IN THE "HOTEL MOM."

But for all animals, as a youngster becomes more independent, there comes a time when it cuts the ties and heads out on its own.

WHAT? IS THIS A HINT?

Some social animals live in groups where "junior" can still keep in touch with the family now and then.

GRUNT

GRUNT

But most animals simply leave home one day and never see or need family again.

'BYE, SON! DON'T BOTHER TO WRITE!

MOST OF THE TIME, INSTINCT SERVES AN ANIMAL VERY WELL. BUT BECAUSE BUILT-IN BEHAVIOUR IS AUTOMATIC, OCCASIONALLY AN ANIMAL MAY END UP DOING THINGS THAT AREN'T TOO HELPFUL.

SOUNDS LIKE THIS MAY GET A LITTLE EMBARASSING...

HEH HEH

RUB RUB

PROBLEMS WITH INSTINCT

For example, penguins have strong instincts to sit on their eggs to warm them until they hatch. But the urge is so powerful, some penguins have been found trying to warm stones, round chunks of ice, and even lightbulbs.

OOPS.

EVEN A BUNCH OF BUILT-IN BEHAVIOURS AREN'T ALWAYS ENOUGH TO DEAL WITH SOME PROBLEMS...

A TARANTULA SPIDER HAS EVOLVED SEVERAL DIFFERENT RESPONSES TO DIFFERENT ATTACKS.

TARANTUL

If poked in the side, the spider will walk away slowly.

A puff of air will make it jump.

If something approaches from the front or above, the spider will raise its front legs and open its fangs.

With these reflexes, the spider can defend itself quite nicely — most of the time.

TARANTULA HAWK

BUT IF IT'S ATTACKED BY A SMALL WASP CALLED A TARANTULA HAWK, NONE OF THESE DEFENSES WORK.

THE SPIDER REARS UP, BUT THE WASP HAS ITS OWN INSTINCTIVE MOVEMENT PATTERNS THAT LET IT SLIDE UNDER THE TARANTULA AND STING IT. THIS PARALYZES THE SPIDER.

It has no chance against the wasp because it has evolved no reflex to stop the attack.

WHAT COMES NEXT FOR THE TARANTULA ISN'T NICE:

THE WASP LAYS ITS EGGS ON THE HELPLESS SPIDER, AND BURIES IT SO ITS BABIES WILL HAVE FOOD WHEN THEY HATCH.

SO INSTINCTS AREN'T PERFECT?

BUILT-IN BEHAVIOURS TAKE A LONG TIME TO FORM, SO THEY ALSO TAKE A LONG TIME TO CHANGE...

... BUT THEY ALWAYS EVOLVE FOR A REASON.

Sometimes an animal's behaviour can seem very strange.

Remember our male three-spined stickleback from page 78? As he's doing his weird zigzag dance for a female, he may suddenly dart off to his nest and swim through it.

At first, scientists called this:

INAPPROPRIATE BEHAVIOUR!

WHY LEAVE THE FEMALE?

WHY GO THROUGH THE NEST?

But then others said:

MAYBE HE'S MAKING SURE THE NEST IS READY FOR THE EGGS. IF IT ISN'T READY, THERE'S NO POINT IN CONTINUING.

AND IF HE DOES CONTINUE, HE'S ALWAYS CALMER AND MORE READY TO MATE.

WHATEVER IT DOES, THIS "WEIRD" BEHAVIOUR IS IMPORTANT TO THE STICKLEBACK.

JUST BECAUSE AN ANIMAL DOES SOMETHING THAT SEEMS STRANGE TO HUMANS DOESN'T MEAN IT'S POINTLESS OR WRONG. HUMANS—INCLUDING SCIENTISTS—DON'T KNOW EVERYTHING ABOUT ANIMALS.

98

BUT MORE OFTEN THESE DAYS "WRONG" BEHAVIOURS DO COME UP BECAUSE THE ANIMAL'S ENVIRONMENT HAS BEEN CHANGED.

THIS DOESN'T MEAN THE ANIMAL IS STUPID OR PRIMITIVE.

Over millions of years, animal species have evolved to fit their surroundings. But over a very short time, humans have changed the environments of many animals.

PARKING LOT

KAKAPO

The kakapo is a large parrot that lives in New Zealand. For millions of years no large predators lived on those islands (only birds could fly there from Australia), so over many generations the kakapo became fat and flightless.

AUSTRALIA

NEW ZEALAND

When the Maori came to New Zealand they cut down forests. Later, Europeans not only cut down a lot more forest, they also brought hungry rats, cats and stoats.

UH-OH.

99

The birds' problem is that, over millions of years, they've lost the instincts for dealing with predators.

IF YOU REALLY SCARED A KAKAPO, IT MIGHT SHOW AN OLD BUILT-IN BEHAVIOUR: RUN UP THE CLOSEST TREE, JUMP OFF, AND TRY TO FLY...

WELL, I CAN GLIDE A LITTLE...

In most cases though, when an enemy approaches a kakapo, it'll just sit there and watch until it's too late.

There are fewer than 50 kakapos alive today, and all but one are living on a tiny island where all of the human-brought predators have been eliminated.

ABSOLUTELY NO RATS, CATS STOATS, GOATS ALLOWED

HUMAN "PROGRESS" IS MAKING LIFE VERY HARD FOR MANY ANIMALS. BUT SOMETIMES AN ANIMAL WILL GET LUCKY, AND CAN ADAPT ITS INSTINCT TO GET A NEW FOOD SOURCE.

WHAT WOULD I DO WITHOUT DONUTS?

For the last 70 years or so, British milk drinkers have had a bit of a problem with titmice. These birds have learned how to peck through the foil on milk bottles to drink the cream.

Many different types of titmice are now doing this. Obviously, this is a learned behaviour. After all, there were no foil-cap bottles until this century.

BUT HOW DO THEY KNOW HOW TO GET THE CREAM? AND WHY DON'T OTHER BIRDS DO IT TOO?

TUFTED TITMOUSE

Pecking and peeling is the way titmice get their food. They sit, peck at a tree branch, and peel away the bark to get at insects. So learning new tricks involving pecking and peeling comes naturally to a titmouse.

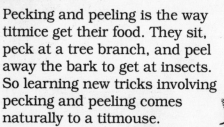

Other birds get their food in other ways, like cracking seeds, so their built-in behaviour doesn't lend itself to the peel-the-foil trick.

101

Titmice are lucky. For most animals, modern-day humans are making their lives much harder. As humans start to intrude into different areas, even defensive behaviours no longer work.

NINE-BANDED ARMADILLO

BOO!

SPROING!

PUFF
PUFF
PUFF

When nine-banded armadillos are frightened...

...they leap almost a metre straight up in the air. This startles the attacker...

...and gives the armadillo time to scurry away through the underbrush.

The problem is that now that there are so many roads (and transport trucks, which drive at night when armadillos are active), the reflex has done the armadillo more harm than good.

USUALLY ARMADILLOS FREEZE WHEN THEY SEE ONCOMING HEADLIGHTS WHILE CROSSING THE ROAD. IF THEY JUST SAT STILL THEY'D BE FINE; THE TRUCK WOULD PASS OVER THEM.

BUT, WITH THE SUDDEN NOISE OF THE ONCOMING TRUCK, THEY JUMP...

Some zoo animals seem to show a lot of strange behaviours. Remember, though, that in the wild these behaviours make a lot more sense.

In the wild, raccoons get a lot of their food from ponds and streams. There, they instinctively paw and search with their hands to uncover fish and insects.

Wolverines in the wild sometimes drink by making a treading or kneading motion with their front paws on marshy ground, to squeeze out water.

Wild cats have an instinct to pluck the feathers of the birds they catch before they eat them.

But if you give a zoo mountain lion or lynx a real bird to pluck and eat, it'll go nuts with the plucking instinct. It goes into a plucking frenzy — feathers, grass, anything pluckable.

Generally, those wild animals that hunt a big meal and then rest do quite well in zoos. They get fed daily, and then can spend most of their time lounging about, which is what they do naturally anyway.

But animals that forage, finding their meals in bits and pieces, don't do nearly so well. In the wild they roam a large area each day, and even though they're given plenty of food in zoos they still have the instinct to search.

LET ME OUT OF HERE!

Even your pet dog shows its ancient instincts. Dogs often turn around as they lie down to sleep. This instinct, it is thought, is an action pattern meant to flatten down a patch of grass for a sleeping nest.

As well, many predators...

...WOLVES, FOXES AND HYENAS, TO NAME A FEW...

...like to roll in dung or other smelly stuff. This may be to disguise their smell so that they can sneak up on prey without being noticed. To the delight of their owners, dogs do this too.

SNIFF SNIFF

WELL, HE CERTAINLY DOESN'T SMELL LIKE A DOG!

SO EVEN IN A WARM HOUSE WITH PLENTY OF FOOD, YOUR DOG'S BEHAVIOUR SHOWS THE RESULT OF MILLIONS OF YEARS OF EVOLUTION.

HUMAN BEHAVIOUR

As usual let's start with reflexes.

106

LET'S SEE. WHAT OTHER BUILT-IN BEHAVIOURS ARE THERE?

YAWN!

Yawning is a mysterious action pattern. In mammals, it may be a reflex, but it happens in many different situations.

Nobody really knows what yawning is for.

TO GET MORE--RRAH OXYGEN!

NO, NO...JAW STRETCHING EXERCISE -- AWWWW...

BEATS MEEEEAH!

DR. MORPHEUS

DR. NARCO

DR. SOMNIA

It's partly social — you're much more likely to do it if someone else yawns first

Strangely, yawning isn't very contagious from kids to grownups.

Just as we've seen in animals, human instincts are connected with basic needs, like feeding, fleeing or living with each other.

GURGLE

GURGLE

SNAP

RUMBLE

Ever start getting cranky just before lunchtime? All animals have built-in food- and drink-seeking behaviours. As your body needs food, you show it by getting grouchy.

107

When you get nervous, many of your body systems suddenly change.

SWEATING STARTS

PUPILS SHRINK

MOUTH IS DRY

HEART SPEEDS UP

STOMACH & GUT STOP DIGESTING

The changes are an automatic response to an emergency. Your brain is preparing your body to escape from what's going on.

When people get bored, they start to do things to arouse their curiosity, even if it's just fidgeting.

TAPPITY TAPPITY TAP

Many mammals explore or fiddle with things to relieve boredom. Captive chimpanzees will work at puzzles for hours, just to figure them out.

TAPPITY TAP TAP

Humans are social animals and many of their built-in behaviours help them to live with others.

A BABY!

HELLO THERE... HIEEE
LOOK AT YOU YOU'RE
SUCH ONE LITTLE
ONE DN'T YC
YES, YOU YES YC
DO! ARE WE OOLIN
YES WE AR
NC

WHAT HAPPENED TO HIS BRAIN?

HIS BRAIN, LIKE MANY ANIMALS' BRAINS, HAS INSTINCTS TO DEAL WITH BABIES. MOST ADULTS AUTOMATICALLY FIND BABIES CUTE, AND WILL PROTECT AND FUSS OVER THEM...

...AND DO THINGS THEY WOULDN'T BE CAUGHT DEAD DOING ANYWHERE ELSE.

GOO GOO GOO GOO GOOOOOOOOOOO!

LOOK AT THAT DOG DEFEND ITS TERRITORY!

GRRRRR

LOOK AT DAD DEFEND HIS CHAIR!

GRRRRR

Just as wild animals and pets try to mark out their turf, so do people.

FOR INSTANCE, MANY FAMILIES SIT IN PARTICULAR SPOTS AT THE KITCHEN TABLE.

Some built-in social behaviours are affected by the group you're with. Humans like to have their own "personal space" that they let only family and friends enter. The size of this space is different depending on the person's culture.

IF THEY CAN'T KEEP THIS SPACE (SAY, ON A CROWDED BUS) THEY'LL MAKE THE SPACE BY NOT LOOKING DIRECTLY AT ANYONE.

Another social behaviour may pop up if you've got a tricky task to do. Often, when you're concentrating on something, you'll stick out your tongue slightly without thinking.

It seems to say to others "don't bother me" or "I'm busy." Gorillas do the same thing. This suggests that the tongue-show is partly built-in.

THE TONGUE IS USED BY YOUNG BABIES TO STOP EATING WHEN FEEDING AT THE NIPPLE...

...OR AT THE PLATE...

PUT!

PUT!

PUT!

PUT! PUT!

This may start to mean, "no more right now." Later, children may begin to tongue-show to send a message to others....

HOCKEY CARDS

For instance, babies instinctively stumble around and babble, but it takes lots of practice to walk without going splat and to talk in sentences.

From toilet training to playing baseball or the violin, learning lets humans pick up and master many skills that they don't know instinctively but may need to survive (this doesn't explain the violin).

Almost all animals can learn. But you don't learn by trying to take in all information...

These things are different for every species....

Chimpanzees learn where and when fruits, roots and termites can be found and eaten, because it's important to them.

On the other hand, leopards don't pay much attention to roots and termites. We all see the world differently.

INSTINCTS GUIDE ANIMALS TOWARD LEARNING THINGS THAT HELP THEM SURVIVE.

THEY'RE THE TOOLS AN ANIMAL USES TO STAY ALIVE...

READING LIST

Animal Behavior by Niko Tinbergen (The Life Nature Library, Time-Life Books, 1965). A look at animal behaviour with an emphasis on experimental studies. Lots of nice illustrations and photographs.

THIS SERIES IS PRETTY OLD, THOUGH, SO SOME OF ITS IDEAS ARE KIND OF DATED.

Animalwatching by Desmond Morris (Jonathan Cape, 1990). Another packed review of animal behaviour with tons of terrific photographs of animals in the wild.

In the Shadow of Man (Collins, 1971), and **Through a Window** (Houghton Mifflin, 1990) by Jane Goodall. The continuing story of the lives of chimpanzees studied by the famous researcher.

Innocent Killers by Hugo and Jane van Lawick-Goodall (Houghton Mifflin, 1970). A loving look at wild dogs, hyenas and jackals, who aren't as nasty as people make them out to be.

Last Chance to See... by Douglas Adams and Mark Carwardine (Stoddart, 1990). A humorously-written book on the very serious subject of the world's rarest animals.

THEY EVEN MENTION US MEGAPODES, EVEN THOUGH WE'RE NOT THAT RARE.

ACTUALLY, THEY **MAKE FUN** OF US MEGAPODES.

Manwatching by Desmond Morris (Jonathan Cape, 1977). An entertaining stroll through human behaviour and culture.

Trials of Life by David Attenborough (Little, Brown, 1990.) Another jogging tour of animal behaviour in nature (again with lots of pictures!). Based on the TV series.

GLOSSARY

AND RELATED TERMS OF INTEREST

action pattern A simple behaviour, set off by a stimulus, made up of a series of actions that follow each other automatically even if the stimulus is taken away.

carnivore Meat-eater (examples: cats, owls, sharks).

conditioning or **paired learning** Changing a behaviour by pairing it with a stimulus again and again. Usually the starting behaviour is fairly simple. For example, a dog drools when it's being fed. If the food is paired with a ringing bell enough times, pretty soon the dog learns to drool at the sound of the bell.

dominance hierarchy or **pecking order** The way some animal groups arrange themselves so that certain members get their way (dominate) over others. Usually rank is determined by fighting or threatening each other.

evolution The gradual change in the looks and behaviour of living things over many generations. Evolution happens because of two things: **variation** and **natural selection**.

foragers Animals that constantly search and rummage around for food (usually small prey or plants).

gland An organ that releases chemicals (called **glandular secretions**) either inside or outside the body. For example, humans have sweat glands and birds have oil glands on their skins; inside you have a pituitary gland that's part of your growth machinery.

herbivore Plant-eater. Examples: rabbits, antelopes, elephants.

insectivore Insect-eater. Examples: shrews, many bats.

natural selection The effect of **variations** that make some animals more likely to survive in their surroundings than others. They'll tend to have more babies than the others, making the new traits more common. A factor in **evolution**.

omnivore Everything (meat and plant)-eater. Examples: dogs, bears, humans.

parasite An animal that lives and feeds on or in another animal (called the **host**). Often the parasite is harmful to the host. Birds like cuckoos are called parasitic because they slip their eggs into other birds' nests, making the host birds do the dirty work of raising the chicks.

predators Animals that hunt other animals.

prey Animals that get hunted.

reflex A simple response produced by a stimulus, like the small kick produced by the tap of a hammer below a kneecap. A reflex can be a defence; for example, the **startle reflex**, when the stimulus of an enemy's very close approach causes the animal to make a sudden move that surprises the attacker.

"selfish" behaviour When an animal does whatever it can to make sure that it survives and has babies, even at the expense of other animals in the group.

social animals Animals that live in groups and interact with others. Some examples are prairie dogs, most monkeys and apes, and ants. Animals that live alone, like tigers and bears, are called solitary animals.

species A group of animals who can and do breed with each other in nature. Usually, different species can't mate or produce babies. A few different species, in captivity, can mate and have babies (for example, horses and donkeys can make mules; lions and tigers can make tiglons), but those animals (mules and tiglons) can't have young themselves.

stimulus Any change in an animal's surroundings (light, noise, touch, taste, temperature, etc. etc.) that causes it to respond (reflex, action pattern, emotion, comment — "ow!"). For some behaviours, the stimulus must always be there for the behaviour to continue. In others, like **action patterns**, it carries on whether the stimulus is still there or not.

variation The way in which all animals of a single species are slightly different from each other depending on the traits they've inherited from their parents. The basis of **natural selection** and a factor in **evolution**.

Note

Dinosaur/bird buffs will notice that the chart on page 23 does not show how birds evolved. This is because the scientists are still arguing about it. Right now, scientists think that birds either evolved from early reptiles (just after the stem reptiles), or from the dinosaurs. Stay tuned!

Speaking of strange behaviour, what about staying up until one in the morning drawing cartoons? Husband-and-wife team **Peter Cook** and **Laura Miye Suzuki** got to know each other this way, working side by side at the same drafting table in the office of their school newspaper. (They were working on degrees in biological psychology at the same time.) When not drawing, Peter practises aikido and plays the guitar and recorder (sort of). In her spare time, Laura plays piano and recorder and composes music. They also play far too many computer games. Bad Peter. Bad Laura. They have recently completed a series of science books called *David Suzuki Asks: Did You Know . . .*